Frogs

Contents

Frog Colors

Some frogs are green.
Some frogs are brown.
Some frogs are orange.
Some frogs are blue.

Some frogs have stripes.
Some frogs have spots.
Some frogs are
hard to see.

Frog Families

Frogs lay eggs.
Tadpoles hatch from eggs.

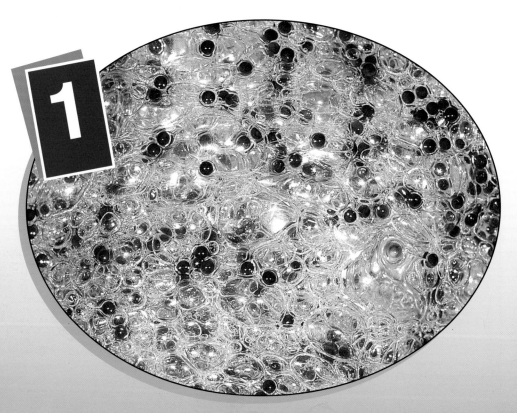

2

A tadpole changes
into a frog.

Frog Homes

Some frogs live in trees.
Some frogs live in ponds.
Some frogs live in tanks.
Frogs live in freshwater.

Frog Facts

Frogs can swim.
Frogs can climb.
Frogs can leap.
Frogs can croak.
Frogs breathe air.

Frogs eat insects.
They blink when
they swallow.
Their eyes help to
push down the food!

Index